Newbridge Discovery Links®

To the Rescue

Debra Lucas

Newbridge

A Haights Cross Communications Company

To the Rescue
ISBN: 1-58273-714-2

Program Author: Dr. Brenda Parkes, Literacy Expert
Content Reviewers: Jim Kanzler, Avalanche Expert, Jackson Hole, WY;
 Randy Brandon, Naturalist and Photographer, Anchorage, AK;
 Mary Marshall, Publications Editor, International Association of Fire Chiefs, Fairfax, VA
Teacher Reviewer: Carmen Alvarez-Rodriguez, Austin ISD, Austin, TX

Written by Debra Lucas
Editorial and Design Assistance by Curriculum Concepts

Newbridge Educational Publishing
333 East 38th Street, New York, NY 10016
www.newbridgeonline.com

Cover Photograph: A firefighter on a ladder battling a blaze
Table of Contents Photograph: An ambulance speeding to the scene of an emergency

Photo Credits
Cover: George Post/SPL/Photo Researchers, Inc.; Contents page: Rafael Macia/Photo Researchers, Inc.;
pages 4–5: Galen Rowell/CORBIS; page 6: Grantpix/Photo Researchers, Inc.; page 7: Todd Maisel/
CORBIS/Sygma; page 8: Mingasson/Liaison Agency; page 9: Courtesy of Elbert Washington; page 10:
Peter Miller/Photo Researchers, Inc.; page 11: Kenneth Murray/Photo Researchers, Inc.; page 12: Bill
Alkofer/St. Paul Pioneer Press/SYGMA; page 13: John Eastcott/Photo Researchers, Inc.; pages 14–15:
Charles Bertram/Gamma Liaison; page 16: Galen Rowell/CORBIS; page 17: Austral/SYGMA; page 19:
William Bacon/Photo Researchers, Inc.; page 20: Chris Rainier/CORBIS; page 21: Jim Evans; page 22:
Chris Rainier/CORBIS; page 23: Brenda Tharp/Photo Researchers, Inc.; pages 24–25: Howard M.
Paul/Emergency!Stock; pages 26–29: Randy Brandon/Peter Arnold, Inc.; page 30: Michal Heron/
The Stock Market

10 9 8 7 6 5 4 3 2 1

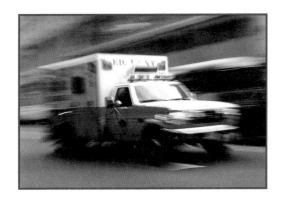

★ TABLE OF CONTENTS ★

A helicopter can rescue people from places that are hard to reach any other way.

Introduction

A casual hike up in the mountains has turned into a life-threatening situation. The hikers cannot find their way back down. They look frantically for a path, as powerful rapids flow hundreds of feet beneath them. One misstep could send the hikers plunging into the rushing water. How will they ever get back alive?

A helicopter has been called to rescue them, but there is nowhere for the helicopter to land. When the hikers are found, two rescue workers are lowered down to the mountain from a **cable**. Quickly and carefully, the rescuers grab the hikers. Soon, one at a time, they are pulled up to safety.

Brave men and women are trained to make daring rescues such as this one. Get ready to meet some of these people and learn about the equipment and the vehicles they use as they come to the rescue.

When the rescuers are lowered down to the ground, the helicopter must remain as still as possible for their safety.

Smoke and Flames

Within minutes of an alarm, firefighters arrive at the scene. But how will they get to a fire on the twelfth floor of an apartment building? Under most conditions, fire ladders only reach seven floors. To rescue someone trapped higher than that, sometimes a firefighter must make a rope rescue. A rope that can hold 9,000 pounds is secured to an object on the roof and attached to a firefighter. Then the firefighter is lowered down to the person trapped at the window or ledge. The firefighter holds on to the victim, and the two of them are lowered to the street.

They could also be lowered to a safer floor, where they are helped into a window by other firefighters.

Cooperation is important for any rescue. Those in the ladder company find people in the building. The firefighters in the **engine company** operate the hoses to put out the fire.

A firefighter directs the powerful blast of water from the hose.

Firefighters battle a blaze at a high-rise building.

All Suited Up

The heat of a raging fire is almost unbearable, reaching 900°F. No ordinary human being can survive in that kind of heat. But from top to bottom, a firefighter is equipped with clothing that can withstand the heat and smoke. Without it, a fire rescue would be nearly impossible.

The helmet is made from a very tough plastic material such as Kevlar. Its plastic visor protects the eyes, and its fireproof hood protects the neck and ears. An air pack and mask help the firefighter breathe despite thick black smoke.

Reflective material wraps around the ankles and wrists of the coat and pants, which are waterproof and heatproof, so the firefighters can see one another in dark or smoky places. The rubber boots are steel-reinforced so nothing can puncture them or crush the firefighters' toes.

A firefighter's entire outfit is called turnout gear, and it can weigh more than 60 pounds!

★ "I WAS THERE" ★

It was the middle of winter when a fire call came in to Rescue Company 2 in Brooklyn, New York. Firefighter Elbert Washington was on the scene right away. Here is his story.

"I quickly ran up six flights of stairs," he says, "and found heavy smoke. Using my iron tool, which is similar to a crowbar, I forced the apartment door open. A closed door keeps the fire from spreading. I had to make sure the door would close again and contain the fire, yet not lock behind me, leaving me trapped.

"The heat was so intense, I dropped to the floor. I heard calls for help. It was dark inside with smoke and I had to feel my way, guiding myself toward the sound. Finally I reached the woman. I knew I had to work quickly to save her life."

The woman inside was Patricia Lane, a New York City police officer. Washington was already exhausted from dashing up six flights of stairs and working his way through the smoke and flames. But he carried her to the floor below the fire and revived her. Thanks to him, she is alive today.

Elbert Washington received a medal for his bravery.

"Another great honor," he said, "is that Ms. Lane and I have been very good friends ever since that day."

The hoses shown here are releasing a series of brief, powerful bursts of water to put out the fire in all areas.

Rescue Tools

A firefighter's act of bravery is priceless to those trying to escape smoke and flames. But firefighters do more than save people and property from fires. They are called upon every day to perform rescues that require other lifesaving skills and equipment.

For example, when someone is trapped inside a car and must get out quickly, firefighters reach for a tool called the **jaws of life**. It works like a giant can opener, and can pry open bent metal and steel, freeing people who are trapped inside a wreck. It is so heavy that sometimes two firefighters need to operate this 50-pound tool!

One rescuer will go inside the car and attach the victim to the backboard, while the others guide it out.

Sometimes the only way to move an injured person without causing further harm is to strap the person to a special kind of **stretcher** called a backboard. The firefighters shown above will remove the victim safely from the car by attaching the person to the backboard. Then they will slowly and carefully pull it out through the window.

Firefighters rescue people from all kinds of disasters that strike a community. They are often the first ones on the scene and the last ones to leave. They help people evacuate their homes during hurricanes, tornadoes, and floods. But even firefighters can't do it all when a community is dealing with a serious flood.

Rising floodwater can damage electrical wires, causing fires to break out.

Too Much Water

It was the summer of 1993. The Mississippi River was overflowing, leaving people with their homes and businesses ruined. People who lived along the river their whole lives couldn't remember seeing the water level so high. In some places the water was rising an inch an hour.

Major floods like this one can create a great deal of damage. Streets can become impassable, fires can break out, and people can become trapped and afraid. Police and firefighters drive boats along what used to be roadways and gather people from their homes and businesses. Trucks make their way through the water, equipped with first aid equipment, life jackets, ropes, and firefighting tools.

But sometimes another kind of vehicle is used. It's called a **hovercraft** and it floats on top of the water.

It is hard to determine where familiar places are when all landmarks, such as trees and roads, are underwater.

Floating on Air

In flooded areas, a hovercraft helps rescue people from their homes or from places of temporary safety on top of roofs, trees, and telephone poles.

A powerful fan forces air to fill an area beneath the craft and a rubber strip called a skirt that goes all the way around it. The air creates a cushion, allowing the hovercraft to float on water. This air cushion also stops the bottom of the craft from hitting and scraping the ground when it moves from the water onto ice or hard ground.

The hovercraft was invented in 1955 by a man named Sir Christopher Cockerell. First he tested his idea using an empty cat food tin inside a coffee can, an industrial air blower, and a pair of kitchen scales. This experiment inspired him to continue his design for a vehicle that could travel on a cushion of air. Since its invention, the hovercraft has performed many rescues that could not have been done otherwise.

But floods aren't the only situations that require water rescues. What if someone is **stranded** in the middle of the ocean?

Hovercrafts are not just used on flooded streets. They can travel over choppy waves at sea, and even over ice or grass.

Help from the Skies

There is nothing but water as far as you can see. The shore is hundreds of miles away. Jagged rocks and powerful surf don't allow even a chance of climbing to safety.

This is where rescue helicopters come in. Helicopters are often used for lifting people out of dangerous situations. A helicopter can travel at high speeds when time is a matter of life and death. It can land on top of mountains where no other type of vehicle can even get close. And a helicopter can hover in one place in the air long enough to let down a lifesaving steel cable called a **winch**.

Helicopter rescues don't always take place in nice weather. They often take place in storms and wind.

Rescue helicopters have first aid equipment onboard to help people during the flight to a hospital.

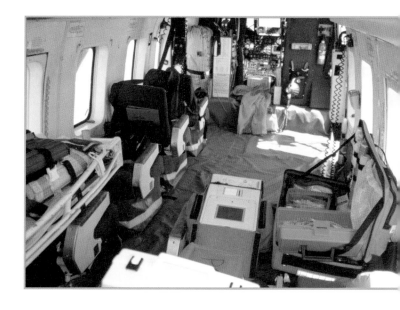

Usually one rescuer is attached to the cable and is lowered down to grab the person who needs to be rescued. Another rescuer, the winch operator, stays inside the helicopter and works the equipment that brings everyone back up safely.

Rescue helicopters are also equipped with all kinds of lifesaving equipment. They carry flotation bags so people remaining in the water can stay afloat. Powerful spotlights light up dark water so that people become visible at night. Some helicopters are built so that the tail can be folded to the side, and the helicopter can be carried on a ship until it is needed in the middle of the water.

Too much water can create flooding. But what happens when the water freezes and turns into an icy monster of falling snow?

Avalanche!

Avalanches are huge, tremendously powerful "landslides" of snow. They usually occur on a mountain, during or after a snowstorm. What most people don't realize is that an avalanche is like a trap, a disaster all set up and waiting to happen. Often, all an avalanche needs to begin is one person's weight moving over the snow.

There are two types of snow avalanches. One kind consists of loose snow that keeps **accumulating** —like a giant snowball—as it slides down the mountain. The other type, a slab avalanche, consists of very compact, dense snow and ice that break away from a mountain in huge masses and roar down it like a runaway train. Both can be frightening and overpowering. So why do some mountain-patrol experts create avalanches on purpose?

An avalanche can cover everything in its path. Most avalanches occur away from places where people ski.

Avalanche Hunters

One way to save people from an avalanche is to prevent it from happening in the first place. It is not unusual to hear explosions very early in the morning, echoing their way across snow-covered mountains. It's the snow patrol, sometimes called avalanche hunters, at work. Using **dynamite** or other small explosives, they break up huge pileups of snow or areas of snow on the mountains that are cracking or sliding. This causes avalanches in controlled settings so they don't take place later and become much larger.

Jim Kanzler has spent more than 30 years studying

avalanches. He has been an avalanche forecaster in the Bridger Teton National Forest in Wyoming. He is skilled at knowing where and when an avalanche might occur. And he also knows firsthand that luck and timing have a lot to do with surviving.

Rescuers train so that they are prepared to save lives in an emergency.

★ "I Was There" ★

Jim Kanzler was on ski patrol with a coworker on a mountain.

"We had spent the early part of the morning creating avalanches so that the slopes would be more stable later on.

"Suddenly, I felt as if I was standing on a white blanket of snow and the entire blanket was moving fast. It just swept me along with it. Then it started to break into huge chunks. I was able to ski off the side of it and escape the slabs that were breaking apart.

But I stood and watched my coworker pushing the snow up with his hands, trying desperately not to get buried.

"Finally, all was quiet. He was covered in snow up to his armpits. I was able to ski over to him and help him out.

"We were very lucky that day. But it shows that even when you think an avalanche won't happen, it helps to be prepared by having done practice drills and carrying the right equipment."

Tools and Practice

People who perform rescues on snowy mountains carry out many practice drills. Sometimes a rescue person pretends to be a victim caught under the snow, and sometimes rescuers use **dummies**. No matter what, they always carry the right equipment. They carry probes, which are collapsible poles that dig into the snow to find people, and shovels to dig victims out.

When rescuers or skiers realize that someone is buried under the snow, they turn their transceivers on to the receive mode.

One of the most important tools carried by rescuers and skiers is a **transceiver**, also called a beacon. It is a small radio device that is strapped onto a skier's clothing, but not hidden in a pocket or pack. The transceiver continuously sends out a series of beeps, and can also receive a beeping signal. The beeps are picked up and rescuers go to the place the sound is coming from, leading them to the victim.

Last but not least, it's important that skiers and rescuers travel in groups of at least two. This is so one person can receive the emergency signal that the other is sending.

Once a victim is found and dug out of the snow, a stretcher is used to carry the person either back down the mountain or to a snowmobile or ambulance that will drive the person safely back.

What happens when someone doesn't have a transceiver? How could he or she ever be found under the snow?

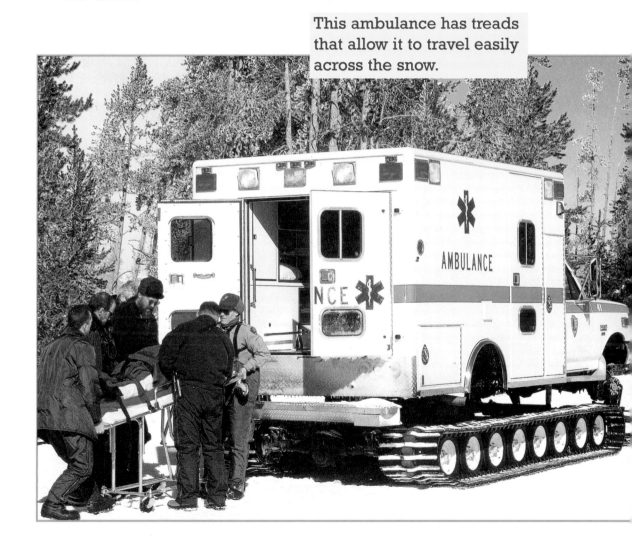

This ambulance has treads that allow it to travel easily across the snow.

A Nose Knows

There is one tool that goes far beyond the capacity of most others for search-and-rescue missions. That tool is a dog's nose. Dogs have the ability and intelligence to be trained to use their keen sense of smell to find someone. They go through months and months of training and, along with their trainers and owners, they are involved in many practice drills. Rescuers and their dogs work as a team to perform successful rescues.

Once dogs find the area where a victim has been buried, they alert the nearby rescue crew by barking and tail-wagging. Then the digging out can begin.

The dogs must pick out an individual's smell through thick layers of snow.

When dogs locate avalanche victims, people can begin the work of freeing them.

Dogs play a major role in rescuing not only people who are caught in avalanches but also those who are trapped under collapsed buildings or lost deep in the woods. But what happens when it's the animals that need rescuing?

These are not trained rescue workers helping the
whales. They are local people coming to their aid.

Animals in Danger

The Inupiat are native people who have lived in the area near Barrow, Alaska, for perhaps thousands of years. They survive by fishing, hunting, and living off the land. One morning while hunting out on the ice, an Inupiat saw three whales crowded in a tiny area of open water. They were gray whales that should have been heading south on their migration to warmer waters. He couldn't understand why they were all staying in this one small area.

Whales are mammals and need to breathe air, so they must find spaces in the water that are not covered by ice. Whales use open areas, called leads, to get to the ocean. But because of huge walls of ice under the sea, these whales had become trapped in one place.

The Inupiat who found them let others know about the whales. Within a few days, freeing the whales had turned into a worldwide rescue effort.

This screw tractor has aluminum tubes that let it float on water once the ice breaks up.

Ice Breakers

More holes needed to be made for the whales so they could breathe as they made their way to the ocean. People all around the world came to photograph, **document**, or help with the rescue.

The ice was so thick that people drove cars over it. One company flew in an ice-breaking machine, called a screw tractor. This vehicle travels on ice by turning large screws on each side. The openings it created did indeed help, but more had to be done. Another company donated chain saws to help the local people cut through the ice. Long poles pushed the broken ice back underneath the surface in order to get it out of the way. But ice re-formed almost as soon as it was taken away. Still, with constant effort, a milelong chain of breathing holes was made.

After many days, two Russian ships called icebreakers sailed toward Barrow and joined the rescue effort. They plowed through the ice until it broke up. Finally, they opened enough water for the whales to swim free to the open ocean.

Those in Barrow worked together and showed many of the traits that professional rescuers have. For all rescues, it's important to act quickly, show caring and concern for those who need help, and of course, be determined not to give up.

The breathing holes were spaced to allow the whales room to swim from one hole to the next.

What Does It Take?

Many types of vehicles transport people who make daring rescues. Some are built to be used in the water, others to be used on land or in the air. As different as they are, they are also alike in that many lifesaving rescues could not be performed without them.

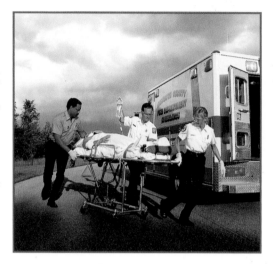

* **A fireboat** is used near the shore when a fire is near a harbor, or on the water when a fire is on a boat at sea. Because it's pumping water directly from the sea on which it floats, it can pump eight to ten times as much water per minute as a fire engine.

* **An ambulance** speeds through the streets with its siren on and lights flashing. The inside is equipped with oxygen, medicine, and all kinds of lifesaving equipment to help a person until the ambulance arrives at a hospital.

* **An air ambulance** is an airplane or helicopter equipped to transport people to a hospital and give them quick medical attention.

★ GLOSSARY ★

accumulating: getting more things or increasing the amount of one thing

cable: a strong length of rope usually made out of steel wires wrapped together

document: to make a record of an event

dummies: objects made in human form that are often used to stand in for people in various activities

dynamite: a powerful explosive

engine company: the crew of a firehouse that responds to a call

hovercraft: a vehicle that floats on a cushion of air so that it may travel over water, ice, or land

jaws of life: a powerful device used to rescue people by prying open or lifting up objects that are hard to move

stranded: lost in a place from which it is difficult to get back

stretcher: a rigid frame with fabric fastened to it, used to get sick or injured people to help

transceiver: a radio that both transmits and receives signals

winch: a rope or cable lowered by a helicopter in order to lift heavy objects

★ INDEX ★

★ WEBSITES ★

For more information about rescues, go to

www.ichiefs.org

www.discovery.com/exp/avalanche/episode1.html

www.weather.com

www.albany.net/~go/apfd/flood.html

www.state.ak.us/local/akpages/FISH.GAME/notebook/
  marine/gray.htm